# THE POWER OF AFFIRMATIONS

by

## JERRY FANKHAUSER, M.S.W.

ISBN: 0-9617006-1-0

Sixth Printing - April 1998

Printed in the U.S.A.
by D. Armstrong Co., Inc.
Houston, Texas

*Dedication*

*This book is dedicated to the Spirit of Creative Love
in all of us that makes us one.*

# Table of Contents

# Chapter I

# WE CAN CHANGE

In working with persons in the counseling process, one of the most common statements made is: "I really have tried to change but nothing seems to work." We try this method and that method, searching constantly, hoping to find something or someone who can give us a concrete way . . . some step-by-step method toward changing our situation and our lives.

Because we feel so helpless in trying to change, we take the line of least resistance and begin blaming others. "If my wife would just straighten up, everything would be fine;" "If my boss weren't so strict, I could do more work;" "If my children would just listen, things would be so much better." When we expect someone else to change so we can change or feel better, we are putting a big limitation on our own personal growth process. We are in the position now in which we have to wait until they change before we can change or feel better. Our life and motivation becomes totally dependent on something or someone other than ourselves. We have turned over the captaincy of our ship to another person.

To begin the change process in ourselves, we must begin to accept two basic concepts: 1) we create our own world and are totally responsible for it; 2) we must see life as a growth process. Only after we have begun to accept these two ideas will we be motivated to search for the way of change for ourselves. Let's look at these two concepts.

Accepting the fact that we create our own world and are responsible for it raises mixed emotions. On one hand we say, we are the result of our parental influence and environment, which is partially true. But we cannot use that as an excuse to blame someone else for our decisions. Just because someone put us down when we were growing up, and we have feelings of inferiority and inadequacy now, does not mean we need to continue in this thought stream. And blaming them only makes the bonds of inferiority and inadequacy tighten because we are enslaved by whatever we hate.

Accepting the fact that we create our own world makes us face the reality that we have made some unwise decisions and we have to admit to ourselves that our lives are open to change. If we can create an unpleasant and unhappy world, we also can create a loving, creative and joyful world, with all its blessings and prosperity.

We tend to see taking full responsibility for ourselves as being negative; that we will be receiving only the consequences of our destructive decisions. That is just one side of the coin. When we accept responsibility for our decisions, we also receive the blessings of our positive decisions. So the world we create is up to us. Taking full responsibility for creating your life is the beginning point of a creative, joyful life.

Eric Butterworth tells a story that describes this point. One night a boy's father brought his boss home for dinner. The boss, a gruff and self-centered man, was a perfect caricature of all the jokes and jests that are made about bosses in general. The young lad stared at him all through the evening. Finally the man asked, "Why do you keep looking at me that way?"

The boy replied, "My daddy says that you are a self-made man." The boss beamed all over at this and proudly admitted that he was. With utmost candor the boy said, "But why did you make yourself like that?"

Each of us is constantly making himself what he is. If we are not satisfied with what we seem to be, then let us remember that we can change ourselves by reshaping our thoughts and attitudes.

The second concept that is basic to change is, life is a growth process. One of the statements I make to persons I am working with in the counseling process is: "You don't have problems and I don't work with people who have problems." After a questioning look I go on to explain. "What you are experiencing is not a problem but an opportunity. You are now aware of a block that you are using to keep more abundant life from coming to you, and this really is an opportunity to move back your limits." We do not have problems but opportunities. The way we have used the word "problem" in our culture implies something endless. Many people feel that life is just one problem after another; and their equation is: life = problems. The Chinese have a beautiful definition of crisis which is "a dangerous opportunity."

Life is growth and part of the process of change seems dangerous because we have to give up and release some things to which we have been attached for many years but, at the same time, it is an opportunity to grow and expand our awareness and consciousness . . . taking in more of God's world.

But change is not easy. We must make the conscious decision to change. Several years ago a person with whom I was working wrote a beautiful parable of how she was at her change point and what was happening. She called it "The Egg That Was Afraid To Hatch."

"Mph! What was that? A stirring inside me? Oh, no! I'll just ignore it, maybe it will go away. Whup! There it is again, ooh! I'm afraid. I think my shell is trying to crack. Oh, please, no.

"Well, I know I'm kind of cramped inside, but what happens if I hatch? I've been watching those other eggs as their shells cracked. Yecocch! Wet, feathery-looking things fall out, all gawky and ugly. No thanks! I'll just remain an egg, smooth and round and uncomplicated . . . I think.

"Or will I? I remember that egg from last year that refused to hatch. It stayed smooth and round alright, but did it smell? It must have been dead inside! Oh! What'll I do? I'm so scared! I don't want to look awkward leaving this shell. I've got pride, same as anyone, but I don't want to die inside, either.

"What will I become if I leave this shell? F-f-f-fried chicken? Waaaah! Somebody help me! I could get killed! I might not be as comfortable outside as I am in here. I might grow up to be one of those fat old clucks with a bunch of noisy chicks to look after, and that looks like a lot of work. But then I might be one of those majestic creatures that flies to the fence post and lets everyone know he's boss. Do you suppose? Wow! I might like that! He's the king of the barnyard, I know! just look at him strut! Gee! I'd like to be a bigshot like that! He isn't afraid of anyone except the farmer.

"The farmer owns all of us, somehow. He decides everything around here, I can tell. If the rooster crows too loudly or long, the farmer knocks him off the fence. Doesn't really hurt him, just wounds his pride. The rooster has a lot of pride, serves him right. Whup! What was that I said about my pride? Well . . . let me see, if I'm too proud to hatch and risk becoming whatever I was meant to be, I could end up awful smelly like last year's egg.

"That did it! I'm getting outa here, ugly or not. Look out world, if you don't like me, that's your problem. I've got to get on with being what I was meant to be. Hey . . . . . . , you gonna hatch."

As we accept these two concepts, we can move on to examining some of the dynamics of this changing, growing process.

# Chapter II

# THE MIND DYNAMICS OF AFFIRMATIONS

As has been said before, the use of affirmations is not magic but a definite process that needs to be understood. In this chapter we will be examining the laws and dynamics behind the successful use of positive affirmation. The following concept has been tried and refined by the author and found very successful in his own life plus has been taught to many of his patients with positive success.

"What you think, you will become; if you think it long enough." This statement is the basis for this whole concept. The process develops as follows:.

THOUGHT
↓
HABIT
↓
BELIEF

We begin with a thought that is planted in the mind and if you think this thought long enough, it becomes a habit. If you habitually think this thought habitually enough, it becomes a belief, something you believe to be true about yourself. Let me give some examples.

If when you were a child the seed thought was planted in your mind that you would not amount to anything and if this were constantly reinforced from external sources, from parents and friends, resulting in our habitually thinking these thoughts, before long we would believe this were true about ourselves. We would begin operating our lives on the basis that this was a truth about ourselves, and eventually we would conduct our lives on the basis this was a truth about us as a person. This would then become part of our growing belief system.

Many of us have had the experience of relating to a person who plays the game "poor me." They are always putting themselves down with statements like: "I never do anything right, nothing ever works for me, no one seems to care, I guess I was meant to be a loser." If we buy into that game, we start playing the "rescuer," trying to convince them that they are not a loser and that they are likeable and lovable. The end result is frustration on the part of the rescuer. You cannot change another's beliefs about himself through persuasion, or by presenting facts. The person playing "poor me" must take responsibility for himself; that he has created this belief and through the understanding and use of mind dynamics, can change the belief to something positive.

Another example was heard in a conversation with a group of teachers. One teacher was telling another,

"I noticed you have Sammy in your class next year. Boy, are you in for it." Of course the other wanted to know about Sammy and was told that he was a difficult child and talked all the time. The seed thought was planted: "Sammy is a difficult child." If that teacher habitually thinks this thought about Sammy long enough, it will become something she believes about him. Before Sammy comes to her class, she has a belief system. What you think, if you think it long enough, becomes a belief.

## THE DYNAMIC PROCESS

Let us now go through the dynamic process of how a thought becomes a belief and the process of how this belief comes into form in our world. The following diagram is an attempt to take an abstract process and put it into picture form.

In diagram No. 1, we see three basic dimensions of the mind: the conscious mind, subconscious mind and super-conscious mind or creative love.

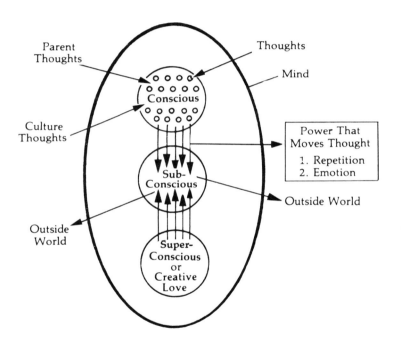

**Diagram No. 1**

Here let me explain each aspect and its functions:

## Conscious Mind

The conscious mind is part of the mind process that observes, thinks and evaluates. The small circles you see in the conscious mind in the diagram are thoughts. The source of seed thoughts within ourselves come from many sources: parents, friends, authority figures, culture, books, etc.

## Subconscious Mind

This part of the mind receives the thoughts from the conscious mind and is the force that puts them into form in our outside world. There is no morality or ethics in this part of the mind. The subconscious mind only carries out the thought that is given to it by the conscious mind. To better understand the relationship between the conscious and the subconscious mind, let me use an analogy.

The conscious mind is like the captain of a ship. He observes the weather, looks at his compass and charts and evaluates what he thinks he should do. He then calls his orders (thoughts) down to the men in the engine room. The subconscious mind is like men in the engine room; they have no idea what is happening outside; they only carry out orders. The ship may be heading toward the rocks but the engine-room men (subconscious) just carry out the captain's orders. There is no evaluation at this level.

Another analogy could be the relationship of a gardener to his garden. The garden is the subconscious mind and the gardener is the conscious mind. The gardener (conscious mind) plants his seeds (thoughts) into the garden (subconscious mind) and whatever is planted will germinate. The soil only produces what the gardener sows and as you sow in your subconscious mind, so shall you reap in your body and environment.

## Power Force that Moves Thought from Conscious to Subconscious

The powers or forces that move a thought from the conscious level to the subconscious level are 1) repetition of the thought; 2) emotion about the thought. You need only one of these elements to move a thought from one level to another. Later, I will give an example of how the process of repetition and emotion works.

## Creative Love

This part of the mind is the essence of you as a person. Some others may use the term superconscious, others may use the terms: Self, creative intelligence, God, etc. Creative love, harmony, and health are forces that are programmed into us and are seeking acceptance and nourishment from us. Creative love is waiting to show us that this is in essence what we are and were created to be.

An example of this is your body. If you do something irresponsible and cut your arm, your body does not stop and think if its going to begin the healing process. It automatically begins because health, healing, and harmony are the essences of creative love moving within the body. When the thoughts coming from the conscious mind into the subconscious mind are in harmony with the essence of Creative Love, we then draw power from Creative Love which gives us added power in creating loving acts in form in our outside world. As more and more positive seed thoughts are planted in the subconscious mind from the conscious mind, there becomes a harmony of energy between the conscious mind and Creative Love and we find our lives becoming a moving flow guided by the essence of Creative Love. We don't have to work at living anymore, but find ourselves "in the flow" of life.

## The Law of Neutrality

Another aspect of the mind dynamic process is the law of neutrality. One of the many laws of physics is that if you have a negative charge and then put a positive charge with it, it will neutralize the negative charge. The reverse is true also. The same is true on the level of thought. If you have a negative thought and you put a positive thought with it, you will create neutralization of the negative thought, and vice versa. This simple law, as will be shown later, is vital when we talk about changing negative thoughts to positive thoughts.

Now that we have an explanation of the different parts of this mind dynamic, let me give you a personal example of how this works.

Several years ago when I began exploring the mind dynamic process, my skepticism was high; it seemed like some form of magic. As the earlier presented ideas began to evolve, I decided to try the process. I had just finished reading Dr. Joseph Murphy's book, *The Power of Your Sub-Conscious Mind,*[1] and he was very much in my thoughts. One day while at work I had an argument with one of my coworkers and found myself very angry and I knew the next morning we were going to have to work out the problem.

That night, while lying in bed, I began thinking of the negative, cutting things I could say to her the next day. My conscious mind contained predominantly negative thoughts. Let's look now at that diagram again:

[1]The Power of Your Sub-Conscious Mind, by Dr. Joseph Murphy, copyright 1979, Prentice-Hall.

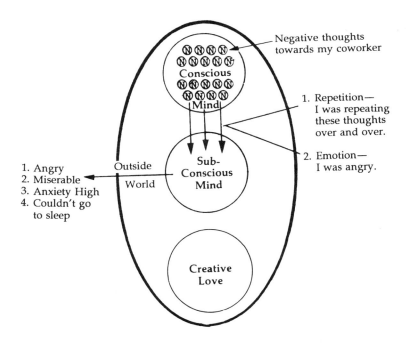

Negative thoughts towards my coworker

Conscious Mind

1. Repetition—
   I was repeating these thoughts over and over.

2. Emotion—
   I was angry.

Sub-Conscious Mind

Outside World

1. Angry
2. Miserable
3. Anxiety High
4. Couldn't go to sleep

Creative Love

**Diagram No. 2**

Through the repetition (constantly repeating these negative thoughts) and emotion (my anger), the negative thoughts moved from conscious mind to the subconscious mind where they were put into form in my world, with the experience of making myself miserable, anxious, and unable to go to sleep. What I was thinking, I was becoming.

At this point I became aware of what I was doing to myself and decided to see if I could change the situation. I decided that if I could create an unpleasant situation for myself, I also could change what I was doing and make it a more positive and healthy climate.

I decided to take one of the affirmations that Dr. Murphy used in his book and test this mind-dynamic process. The affirmation chosen was "May the richest of the blessings of life be with her." I began repeating this over and over to myself. Of course as I began repeating this affirmation, the thoughts in my conscious mind were predominantly negative, but what I was doing was beginning the process of neutralization. As I kept repeating this affirmation, the negative thoughts were being neutralized (see Diagram No. 3) until the balance of power in the conscious mind moved from negative thoughts to the positive thought, "May the richest of the blessings of life be with her." The neutralization process took about fifteen minutes. As the balance of power changed, now the message going to the subconscious mind was positive and my outside world started changing and I was able to calm down and go to sleep.

Also, I was drawing added power from the Creative Love part of my mind because this thought was in harmony with Creative Love.

The same process I used to make myself miserable I used to create a positive atmosphere within myself. Keep in mind that this had nothing to do with whether I liked or disliked her at this time. The purpose was to create a positive climate within myself.

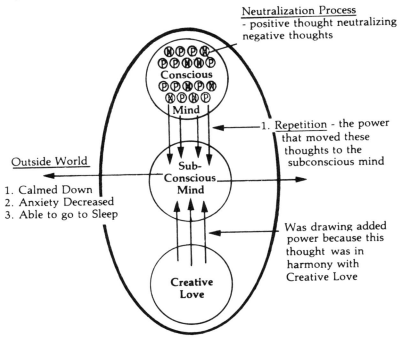

Diagram No. 3

The next morning I repeated the same positive affirmation all the way to work and we sat down and worked out the problem in fifteen minutes. She did not change but what changed was my attitude and the climate within myself. I had, through this process, lowered my own emotional fog level where I could communicate with her and not react to her. If I had gone into that meeting with all the negativity from the night before, we might still be there.

Again this process had nothing to do with liking her; rather I was seeking to take full responsibility for my thoughts and through this mind dynamic, change my inner climate where communication could take place. There was no magic but the understanding and use of the law of the mind. In short, if I could create a miserable climate within myself, I also could create a positive climate within myself.

At this point I would like for you to experience this dynamic through the use of an exercise. Sit comfortably and take two deep breaths and release them slowly. Close your eyes and slowly and gently begin repeating to yourself, "I am peaceful and calm, I am peaceful and calm." Just keep repeating this to yourself for three to five minutes. If during the repeating of this thought you find yourself thinking other thoughts, do not fight the thoughts, but just be aware you are thinking them and move slowly back to repeating, "I am peaceful and calm." Begin the exercise.

Now that you have completed the exercise, let's look again at what happened. When you began the exercise, you probably were not as calm as you are now; so there were other thoughts that were predominant in your mind. When you began repeating, "I am peaceful and calm," you were not immediately calm but you started the neutralization process. As you continued the repetition (remember this was one of the forces that moves thought from conscious to subconscious mind) the balance of power in the conscious mind was changed to where the predominant thought now going to the subconscious mind was, "I am peaceful and calm." In your outside world, you began calming down and feeling relaxed. Again, you drew power from Creative Love. This is a simple but effective exercise that can be used at anytime. The above dynamics can help us to understand what is going on when we use the affirmation process and give us clues as to why our affirmations may not be as effective as they could be.

# Chapter III

## STEPS IN CHANGING OUR THOUGHT CLIMATE

Now that we have an understanding of the mind dynamic process and the way that thoughts are transformed into events and experiences in our world, let's move on to a step-by-step process of how we change our negative thoughts to positive thoughts.

The first step in changing negative thoughts to positive thoughts is awareness. Until we are aware of what negative thoughts are operating in our minds, we are victims of these negative thoughts and they are in control. From birth we have had many seed thoughts planted in our minds and through the earlier described process have come to accept them as the truth about ourselves. Not knowing how to change these thoughts we have just accepted them and have conducted our lives as if they were true.

One way we can become aware of these basic beliefs about ourselves is to write down our thoughts when we are experiencing fear, depression, anger and loneliness. These down times are being reinforced by all of our basic negative thoughts. Some examples are: "I will never amount to anything," "No one ever listens to me," "Why try, no one cares," "Life is just a grind," "I always get hurt," "Life is just one problem after another." As we seek to become aware of our thoughts, we will be amazed at how much negative thought is going on inside of us.

Another simple thought awareness exercise is to carry a pocket notebook with you and write down negative thoughts that come to you during the day.

To experience the steps in changing thought process, stop now and write down three negative thoughts you frequently say to yourself. For example: "I am too impatient," "I blow up too easily and can't handle anger," "I always get manipulated," etc.

The second step in changing negative thought to positive thought is to take each negative statement you have written and out beside it write a positive statement. This step is where much confusion can take place because we must be sure the new statement is positive.

Here let me speak to the source of this confusion. Don't be discouraged if you found it difficult to think of a positive thought about your negative statement. I have found in helping people with this step that there seems to be a mind block in thinking of a positive statement. In our culture we are programmed to think defensively, seeking only to make sure something negative doesn't happen to us with the false assumption that if we can keep negative things from happening to us, we will automatically have the positive. This is not true. Many people will say, "I don't want to be like my mother," "I don't want to be like my dad," "I don't want to be like my husband," etc. They spend so much time not being something, they never are anything. Others will say, "I don't want to do this or I don't want to do that," and consequently they never do anything. Our energy is then directed toward not being or doing anything, just being sure nothing negative happens to us. I once asked a person if she was happy and her reply was, "I don't know, but I'm not unhappy." When you examine this statement you find an interesting observation. This person is not happy, which we could say is at one side of the scale and she is not sad, the other side of the scale, but where is she? She is not unhappy which is another way of saying she is nowhere, just living life defensively. Living life defensively only creates a vacuum. Let me paraphrase a biblical story that illustrates this point.

Once upon a time there was a man who had an evil spirit in his house. It was causing him much misery, so he decided to rid himself of that spirit with the hope that once the spirit was gone, he would be a happy man and live a prosperous life. He obtained the services of a very wise man in his town. The seer told him that two things needed to be done, but would only give him the first task; informing him that he would need to return for his final instructions. He now knew how to drive out the evil spirit, and went home and swept his house clean, room by room, from cellar to attic. The evil spirit left and the man sat in his easy chair satisfied that the problem was solved. He was so satisfied that he forgot to return for his final instructions. Several weeks later the evil spirit was walking by and decided to peek in the window to see who was living in the house. Much to his surprise, he saw nothing but bare rooms that were very clean. Seeing the emptiness of the house and being without a home, he moved back in; this time bringing several of his cronies with him, each with ten servants and a chauffeur.

We operate on the basis of "don'ts" and "thou shalt not's" so much of the time and spend all our effort worrying about keeping negative aspects out of our lives that no time is spent putting new furniture in our houses. We clean and clean our house, but still feel the emptiness.

There is an old comic strip that pictures this dilemma. Those comic-strip characters were called the "Goops," mythical characters created by Gellet Burgess to help parents teach good manners to their children. They were supposed to illustrate for children what they were NOT to do in order to be well mannered. The Goops threw ink bottles at the walls, ate with their fingers, broke dishes, soiled the tablecloth, and did all kinds of things which would make Dennis the Menace look like an angel. The moral for the children was, "Don't be a Goop." But the idea backfired. Parents discovered that the distressing behavior of the Goops, instead of arousing a moral protest in the youthful readers, suggested some fascinating possibilities that could educate their children with continuous negative suggestions.

The Greeks have a story that may give us some direction. It is about Ulysses and the Sirens who sang so sweetly that sailors could not resist steering toward their island. Many ships were lured upon the rocks and men forgot home, duty and honor as they flung themselves into the sea to be embraced by arms that drew them down to death. A man could manage to sail by the Sirens safely only if he could say "no" to the Sirens. But finally they learned a better way to save themselves; they took on board their own, better music. When Orpheus sang, who bothered to listen to the Sirens? We must move beyond just saying "no" to negative thoughts and bring some new music (positive thoughts) into our lives.

Changing negative thought to positive thought is not just saying "no" to the negative. At one point in my life when I started using affirmations I experienced this dilemma. I was using the affirmation, "I don't like my impatience," thinking this was a positive way to change. One day while telling a friend about the fact that nothing seemed to be changing, he said to me, "That's not a positive thought. You are just telling your impatience 'no' and putting nothing in its place." He was right; I was thinking defensively. His suggestion was the positive affirmation, "I love patience."

Being sure we are making a positive statement is a very important part of this process. Let me use the examples in step one to illustrate the point. "I am impatient," could be changed to "I love patience," or

"I am a patient person." "I blow up too easily and can't handle my anger," could be, "I take responsibility for my feelings and allow others to take responsibility for their's," or "I am positively open and honest with my feelings." Manipulation comes when we are not aware of our own feelings and not taking responsibility for them.

Now to continue our exercise, take the three negative thoughts you have written and change them to short, simple positive statements.

Step three is repetition and emotion. Remember the power that moved your negative thoughts from the conscious mind to the subconscious mind was repetition and emotion, so we are using the same dynamic to move positive thought from one level to the other. Just as negative thoughts maintain their power by repetition and emotion, positive thoughts work the same way. The third step is to begin repeating each of your new positive affirmations at least ten times during a quiet time in the morning and in the evening and anytime during the day they come to mind. You are now beginning the neutralizing process.

Repeating these new affirmations is only half the process. We must repeat each one with feeling and emotion, feeling the thought inside ourselves. To repeat the thoughts casually will do no good; you must have the power to move them to the subconscious level. The power is your emotion in each statement. You have started the neutralizing process, planted the seed and each day as you continue, you nourish the seed thought. Again let me say, this is not magic and it does take time and effort. It has taken much time and effort to create your negativity; it will take time and effort to reverse the process.

Now that you have begun, don't get in a hurry for results. Begin and continue. If you become impatient, it will be like planting a seed in your garden and going out each day, digging it up to see if it has grown any.

Let me suggest a simple procedure to follow each morning and evening. You might go through the exercise right now. Sit or lie comfortably and begin repeating very slowly, "I am peaceful and calm." After five to ten minutes or when you feel yourself calm, begin repeating each new affirmation slowly and with emotion and out loud if possible at least ten times. After you have repeated each affirmation ten times, go back to repeating, "I am peaceful and calm," for two or three minutes. If you do this exercise each morning and evening you will have started the change process. Let me put this exercise in a simple outline form.

1. With eyes closed, begin repeating, "I am peaceful and calm," for five to ten minutes.
2. Repeat each of your three new affirmations ten times with feeling.
3. Conclude exercise with repeating, "I am peaceful and calm," for two to three minutes.

Let me add one thought about results. The neutralizing process takes time and the results will usually begin to happen in a subtle manner. Let me give a personal example. When I began working on my impatience using the affirmation, "I love patience," the results did not come soon or dramatically. It was a month and a half later after consistently, morning and evening, affirming this thought that I noticed a change. I was in a meeting that was very frustrating. In the past my impatience would have been, let us say on a numerical scale, about 100. At that moment I found myself responding about 75 on the scale. It was a noticeable change. Although I was still feeling some impatience, I knew the neutralizing process had been working and the balance of power about my impatience was shifting. It took time and consistent effort.

# Chapter IV

# HOW TO ORGANIZE YOUR AFFIRMATIONS

Organizing and structuring your affirmations help to channel energy into these thoughts in an orderly manner, measuring the focusing power of that energy. If our life is orderly, then we use less energy and can get more accomplished. It is the same with organizing your affirmations. Let me suggest a structure that can give order and direction to your affirmations.

## Step 1

As was suggested earlier, begin the process with five to ten minutes of relaxing and calming down using the affirmation, "I am peaceful and calm." Repeating this thought can create a climate that enables us to slow down the mind to where it can focus clearly on the affirmations.

## Step 2

Select one general affirmation to help create an overall climate in the mind, an affirmation that centers around a basic truth about life. Let me give some examples: "There is one presence and one power in my life, God, the good, Omnipotent," "I am love, I am loving," "I am in the divine flow of life," etc. Choose one that is personal to you.

## Step 3

In this step select two releasing affirmations. As was mentioned earlier, releasing is an important part of the process. If we do not release a person or situation or fear, etc., then we are continually expending energy, keeping it alive in our mind. Remember anything we will not release, we are enslaved by. You are a slave to any person you hate and will create only hate within yourself. When you release the hate, you open the creative and positive channels so that the love can flow through you once again.

To release means to face a person or situation honestly and when we begin using a releasing affirmation, we will find ourselves reexperiencing some of the pain and hurt that has been harbored. Let me illustrate this process. Many of us have internal boils. These boils represent events and situations that have been painful and yet never have been allowed to heal. So we carry these sensitive areas around inside and when a present situation happens that is similar to one of our inner boils, we not only react to what is happening in the present, we touch that boil and find ourselves experiencing the pain of all past experiences.

You might say we have inner sensitive buttons that start a projector which reruns past films of the same experience.

We need to be aware of the boils, go in and lance them, squeezing out the poison (releasing) and allowing the air to begin the healing process.

As you begin your releasing affirmations, you will find yourself experiencing some of the past feelings plus you will become sensitive to present situations that are similar to the source of past hurts.

Let me illustrate this point. A woman that I counseled over a period of time had many past experiences (boils) of people making her feel guilty. As she became aware of this fact about herself and started the releasing of those people—especially her mother—she made the following comment: "I really am sensitive to people making me feel guilty, and it seems now as I am releasing these persons and situations, I am running into this problem with everyone I meet." What was happening? She was becoming aware of the degree and intensity of that problem, and also the length of time she had been into that game. As she continued the releasing process, she was more aware of how long it had been going on. Releasing always makes us more aware of what needs to be released and changed. As she continued to release, she was more aware now of that problem and saw it in relation to all those people with whom she had been playing this game. Her basic affirmation was in reference to her mother; so as her awareness and releasing continued, she was able not to buy into the game as much and take more responsibility for herself. Every time she was able to catch this game in operation and deal with it in a firm but kind way, she was releasing more of the past poison and found that her present relationships also were improving.

The second part of the releasing statement is to end the affirmation with a positive thought. You have released and let go; now you need to draw something to fill that space. The woman mentioned above used the affirmation, "I release my mother to her highest good." Here she was releasing, neutralizing and affirming something positive in one statement.

Not only can we use releasing in reference to persons but for specific personality changes we want to make. Let us assume you have a fear of the lack of money. Of course if you let this fear thought be predominant, you will have no money. An affirmation that could be used to work on this fear is: "I release my fear of lack and accept the abundance and prosperity of God." If you have problems with dependency or feeling obligated to others, you could use: "I release my fear of dependency and obligations and accept the freedom and responsibility of God."

A good way to find what you need to release is to make a list of your fears and then pick two of them that are the strongest and make a releasing affirmation about them. Why not do that right now? Also I will expand on the releasing process later on in the book.

## Step 4

Choose two positive affirmations that describe what you want to develop in your personality. Here you might write down the characteristics you desire for yourself. Now pick two and make statements about them. For example, "I am a self-confident person," "I love patience," "I am expressing my feelings in an open, honest and responsible way," "I am taking responsibility for my feelings and allowing others to take responsibility for their feelings," etc.

## Step 5

End your list of affirmations with one or two affirmations for someone else. It is important to remember when blessing another person that you see them as whole and complete. You could use the affirmation, "I see (name) as whole and complete with all strength and power to make his/her life happy." Many of us have been taught to send love to another person, but sending love implies that the other person lacks something and we can fill that lack. The other person is already created love so how can we give him something he already possesses? The other person needs nothing but to accept what is already present within him. The way we can bless them is to see them whole and complete and this helps them look inside for their own strength.

Pick one or two people and affirm they are whole and complete.

## Step 6

Close with just sitting and being quiet . . . allowing yourself to experience the joy of inner peace and harmony. Repeating, "I am peaceful and calm," quietly would be helpful.

An example of how you could set up your own affirmation process could be as follows:

1. "I am peaceful and calm." (five to ten minutes)
2. General affirmation: "I am love, I am loving." (repeat ten times with feeling)
3. Releasing affirmations: "I release my mother to her highest good and myself to my highest good." "I release my fear of lack and accept the abundance and prosperity of God." (repeat each ten times with feeling)
4. Positive affirmations about your personality: "I am a self-confident person." "I love patience." (repeat each ten times with feeling)
5. Blessing affirmations: "I see (name) whole and complete with power and strength to take charge of their situation." "I see (name) with strength and courage to make their life happy and joyful." (repeat ten times with feeling)
6. Sit quietly, repeating, "I am peaceful and calm"; then stop all thinking and just enjoy the inner peace.

Earlier in this book I suggested another order for using affirmations. Pick the one that seems best for you.

The six steps can give you an ordered structure for your affirmation process, focusing your mind energy in a positive direction.

# Chapter V

# RELEASING IS EXPERIENCING

Because releasing is so vital to the process of growth, I want to expand on what I said earlier.

Beginning to use our affirmations is only the first step in the change process. Affirmations are not magic. Declaring our affirmations consistently is like priming the pump. These affirmations will immediately begin challenging the belief system on which we are presently operating. The old beliefs will not let go easily but will create resistance. The resistance is usually experienced in the form of doubt and fear . . . telling you to go no farther, "Stop doing these affirmations." Sometimes we may feel that we are dying and, in truth, a part of us is dying—our old self based on false perceptions.

We must accept the fact that resistance will be part of the changing process. The healthy way to deal with the resistance is to just experience it. Fighting the resistance only gives it more power. Non-resistance to what we are experiencing is the key to releasing. Releasing is not an intellectual or mind experience. The mind only helps the process begin.

Because we have operated our lives on a belief system that has not worked, we have accumulated the results of those perceptions: much pain and hurt. Suffering is caused by repressed pain that has its source in perceptions and beliefs that have never worked. But we keep trying them over and over and from this fruitless effort we accumulate pain that has never been released. For example, we have accepted certain perceptions and beliefs from birth about the way relationships should work, and we accept this as truth. We go through relationship after relationship faithfully following in the same beliefs, and always end up frustrated and confused. From each experience we have pain and suffering. It is not until we realize that our belief system does not work that we begin to transform our suffering into pain and release it. This process begins with the use of affirmations which is a verbal declaration of seeking a new perception.

Before the new affirmations can become effective, there is a period of experiencing the results of the old perceptions. For example, if I am affirming having inner peace, then before this becomes a reality I must begin to release those beliefs and experiences that have created conflict and prevented my inner peace. This does not happen all at once. As we are willing to release the past pain, we will become open to the experiences of the new affirmations and perceptions. This is usually experienced in what *A Course In Miracles*[2] calls a Holy Instant. This is an instant when we experience the truth about ourselves. As we are willing to continue to release the old perceptions, consistently affirming our affirmations, we experience more of these Holy Instants until our experience and our affirmations are one and the same.

[2] **A Course in Miracles**, copyright 1975, Foundation for Inner Peace, Glen Ellen, California.

When we are experiencing the pain of release, we allow ourselves to go into the pain, become the pain. The fear at this point is that we will never come out of it or become stuck. Let yourself just experience it. You may find yourself crying, angry or fearful, but allow yourself to go on through it.

Many persons have been taught that if you go into the experience of fear, anger, etc., you are reinforcing it. This is not true. The only way to reinforce fear, anger, guilt, etc. is to think about it. Thinking about our fear is what gives fear energy. Experiencing the fear inside ourselves is to release it. Remember, the only way out is through.

Two suggestions that will help in the process are: (1) write down what you are feeling; (2) call a friend who will be supportive to you and share your experience. The writing and sharing will help speed up the process. Remember, you will be going through this many times. Many people have the illusion that you experience release just once or twice and you have completed the process. This is not true. If you were to release all of the past hurts at one time, you would literally blow a mental fuse. For example, picture a person who has boils all over his body and a doctor walks in and says we are going to lance all of these boils and squeeze out the poison at the same time. I doubt if anyone of us would do this because it would be too painful and overload our physical system. It would be the same with release all past hurt and pain. It would be too much for us.

The healing process is a gentle process. We all have within us a healing force that knows the most gentle and loving way to release the past pain and suffering so as not to overwhelm us. If we are patient and willing to listen to our own healing power, our releasing will happen in this gentle and loving manner.

The following is an analogy I use with my patients. When we finally accept the reality that our beliefs and perceptions do not work, we see that our house is full of garbage. Our life literally stinks. Releasing begins when we decide to clean house, but we don't clean it all at once. We clean a little out, then rest. But remember, as we clean it out we are making room for new furniture, new experiences. This process may go on for some time, but each time we release past pain and suffering, we are moving back our limits to where we can take in more life as it was intended to be. We continue until the house is clean and all corrections are made.

Once you accept releasing as a vital part of the discovery of who you are, the growth process will speed up. Releasing means moving your blocks out of the way to discover the real truth about you; that you are Creative Love. The more we open ourselves to this truth, the more willing we are to release the pain and suffering of the past. We sense the truth about ourselves and releasing then becomes an accepted process of observing more of this truth.

# Chapter VI

# RELEASING IS FORGIVING

If we are to release another person, we need to understand what is happening and what we are attempting to do. Releasing is forgiveness so when we release someone we are also forgiving him/her. Forgiveness does not mean that someone has done us wrong and now we are forgiving him/her. That is not forgiveness. When you forgive another person you are saying, "I forgive you for not being the way I wanted you to be and I release you and let you go." Forgiving and releasing are taking back our projections of what we wanted the other person to be and, in doing this, we free that person and ourselves. Remember when you begin releasing and forgiving, you will begin confronting those needs you have had for someone to be a certain way and act in a certain manner. This can produce a sense of freedom but also a sense of abandonment. This process will bring to light the games you have played and you can begin to see the source of your problems. Giving up the way we wanted another person to be points us in the direction of discovering our inner power and strength.

If we want to begin the forgiving and releasing process in reference to a specific person, the following affirmation can be used.

I forgive (name of person) for not being the way I wanted her/him to be and release her/him and let her/him go.

Do this affirmation every morning and evening and anytime you think of the person.

# Chapter VII

# THE MISUSE OF AFFIRMATIONS

Affirmations are like specific prescriptions for certain aspects of yourself you want to change. When a physician gives you a prescription, it is directed towards some specific physical ailment. Many persons with whom I have worked complain that affirmations do not work and one of the major reasons is because all of their affirmations are of a general nature, none are specific. There is a place for a general affirmation about life and yourself of which we will discuss later, but to make all affirmations general transforms the affirming process into a denial mechanism. Secretly, we are hoping that if we say them long enough, we won't have to deal with what we are denying.

I remember a woman who had been affirming, "I am drawing to me a man who will make me happy," and she was wondering why no one was asking her out. When the suggestion was made to her that she needed to forgive and release her ex-husband, her immediate reply was, "Oh, I'll never forgive him; he really did me dirty." This woman was using the affirmation to deny what she needed to deal with in her life, and, as was told to her, the reason she never got dates was because she still had a man in her life (her ex-husband), and she was maintaining that relationship on the thought level by giving her hurt feelings energy. When she went on a date, there were really two men and not one. Also in her affirmation she was asking someone else to make her happy and no one can make another person happy except that person; and if we expect someone else to take responsibility for our happiness, we have copped out on ourselves. This woman was using her affirmation to deny what she needed to see in herself, hoping that it would just go away.

Another way we can misuse affirmations is to have too many going at the same time. I have seen people who have come in with pages and pages of affirmations and trying to do them all, or persons who begin new affirmations each week, discarding the affirmations of the preceding week. Using affirmations in this manner can become laborious and a burden. We may feel that a volume of affirmations is bound to have a heavy effect. This mind-set comes from our culture and says that volume and amount are most important; quantity, not quality. Yes, we may find a heavy effect by using a great many affirmations, but the weight is only a burden. Many people just go around planting seed thoughts but never take time to water and nourish these new plants, so they soon die.

Another form of misuse is to affirm a new thought without needed action to bring it into form.

A man once told me, "I've been using an affirmation about finding a better job but nothing has happened."

"Have you been looking and reading in possible areas," I inquired?

"Oh no, it will come if I wait long enough."

He is expecting magic to happen. There are affirmations about certain things that need action beyond just the affirming process and failure to follow up with this action can mean the person is not really willing to take responsibility for making this happen. Affirmations operate under certain laws and if we do not follow these laws the results will not be forthcoming.

Working at affirming is another misuse of this process and only creates energy blocks. Working at affirming is like working at trying to go to sleep, you only make the situation more frustrating. As has been said before, quieting yourself down is vital to maximum efficiency of the process. Using the "I am peaceful and calm" exercise begins to create a quiet climate and tells the mind what you want to do for the next few minutes. In other words, it gives a direction to the mind and focuses the energy toward a specific goal. If we immediately begin our affirmations without calming ourselves, then we only add new thoughts to thoughts already going on in our mind and this lowers the effectiveness of the affirmations by diffusing the energy. At this point, we feel that we are working at affirming.

One last misuse of affirmations is to expect instant results. The results may come quickly but to constantly be looking for results is like planting a seed and going out each day and digging it up to see if any growth has taken place. We must begin and continue. When we regularly and consistently do our affirmations without anxious expectation, and put our faith in the mind dynamic process, results begin to occur.

# Chapter VIII

# SITUATIONAL AFFIRMATIONS

Along with going through the six steps each morning and evening, there are times when we need situational affirmations. If you are having an important meeting coming up in a few days, you might want to have an affirmation for that meeting so as to help create a positive climate within yourself. "The meeting on Tuesday will be a positive experience for me," could be an example. This does not mean that there may not be problems but you will be creating your own personal atmosphere and attitude for that meeting. Many businessmen with whom I have worked use a positive affirmation before seeing each client. School teachers who have learned this method use it before school each day to prepare their own mind climate. One doctor uses the "I am peaceful and calm" before he goes into surgery. Some housewives use affirmations before cleaning house so they can minimize their negative attitude toward that task and not end up feeling completely frustrated.

Situational affirmations can help keep the neutralizing process going plus creates a healthier climate for a specific situation.

# Examples of Affirmations for Specific Situations

The following statements are just examples to help you begin using affirmations. You may use these affirmations but it is suggested that you move toward developing your own. There is more power in your personal affirmations because it comes from your efforts and your own creative energy. The following examples will help you get started.

## Affirmations About Who and What We Are

I am love and I am loving.

I am the spirit of love, joy, and peace.

I am a light of love that shines in the world.

The Father of love and I are one.

## *Affirmations About Fear*

I release my fear of _____ and draw to me the joy and peace of God.

There is nothing to fear.

The peace of God is with me now.

(Fear is really our best friend because it lets us know where we don't want to be and when we experience it we are reminded of what we really want, inner peace. We might thank our fear for letting us know we aren't where we want to be at that moment.)

## *Affirmations About Loss of Job*

I release my old job and draw to me the most perfect job for me now.

God is guiding me to the most creative job for me.

## *Affirmations About Anger*

I am never upset for the reason I think.

I release my anger and choose peace.


## *Affirmations About Loss of a Relationship*

I release _____ to their highest good
and myself to my highest good.

The loss of this relationship is an opportunity to learn
more about myself.


## *Affirmations About Being Free*

I am free; I take charge of my own life.

I am free; life is filled with joy and peace.

I am free to be what God created me to be, Love.

# Affirmations About Conflict

In my defenselessness my safety lies.

I have the power and strength to handle this conflict in a loving way.

I choose peace instead of this.

I am hurt by nothing but my thoughts.

# Affirmations About Death of a Loved One

I thank you (name) for being an important part of my life, and I now release you to your own unfoldment.

# Affirmations About Expressing Feelings

I express my feelings in a healthy and responsible way.

My feelings are okay. I express them with wisdom and clarity.

## *Affirmations About Feeling Inadequate and Powerless*

God is the strength in which I trust.

I am whole and complete and all loving power is available to me at anytime.

God goes with me wherever I go.

(You could also use one of the affirmations about who and what you are.)


## *Affirmations About Feeling Lost and Rejected*

I affirm this experience as an opportunity to break through to my own inner peace.

I open myself to being found.

My worth is established by God.

## Affirmations About Guidance

I am open to the guidance of the love of God that flows through me.

God's wisdom and love are guiding me in all things.

I will step back and let Him lead the way.


## Affirmations About Healing

The healing power of God is moving through me now.

I open my mind and body to the healing power of God. My healing is my inner peace.


## Affirmations About Loneliness

I venture forth knowing that God is with me.

I cannot be alone if God is with me.

The assurance of God's love is with me now.

## Affirmations About Health

I give myself the gift of good health.

I feed my body and mind in a loving and responsible way.

## Affirmations About Peace Within

I am the peace of God.

The peace of God flows through me now.

I am peaceful and calm.

The peace of God is shining in me now.

## Affirmations About Prosperity

I release my fear of lack and accept the abundance and prosperity of God.

I am drawing to me the prosperity of God on all levels of my life.

# CONCLUSION

What has been suggested in this book is just a starting point. It can work for you if the effort is made. It has worked for me and for those who have taken it seriously. It is not magic but a way to help grow and expand yourself as a person and to open yourself to the abundance of life that is yours.

MR. JERRY FANKHAUSER, M.S.W. is in private practice as a psychotherapist in Houston, Texas. Along with doing individual, marital and family therapy, he also conducts workshops across the country in the area of personal growth and development. He is a member of the American Association for Marriage and Family Therapy and the American Society of Group Psychotherapy and Psychodrama.

Mr. Fankhauser has had several of his articles published in professional journals and also has written four other books, *From A Chicken to An Eagle, Everybody is Your Teacher, The Way of the Eagle,* and *The Process of Waking Up.*

In his writings and in his practice, Mr. Fankhauser brings together the spiritual and psychological aspects of the person and sees the result of the merger to be spiritual psychotherapy.

If you wish to contact the author personally, he may be reached at the following address:

Mr. Jerry Fankhauser, M.S.W.
7676 Woodway, Suite 380
Houston, Texas 77063
(713) 787-9057